Victorian & Edwardian

COTSWOLDS

from old photographs

1 'Old Cotsaller', the archetypal countryman with smock and neckerchief

Victorian & Edwardian

COTSWOLDS

from old photographs

David Viner

B T Batsford, London

This volume is dedicated to My Mother
In my Father's memory

ISBN 0 7134 3496 1

Phototypeset by Servis Filmsetting Ltd, Manchester
and printed in Great Britain by
The Pitman Press Ltd, Bath
for the publishers
B. T. Batsford Ltd
4 Fitzhardinge Street
London W1H 0AH

Contents

Acknowledgements

This album of photographs owes much to the generosity of a great many individuals, whose response to my enquiries was invariably one of interest and pleasure in being asked to make a contribution to a volume of this kind. It is therefore a particularly pleasant task to be able to thank all those whose material is reflected here and indeed others whose photographs for one reason or another have not been included.

The collections at the Corinium Museum at Cirencester and the Cotswold Countryside Collection at Northleach include an historic photograph archive for the Cotswold District Council area and most of the photographs in this album have been copied with permission for inclusion in the archive for preservation.

Corinium Museum, Cirencester: 2 (Miss K. Tucker, Cirencester); 8 (Rosemary Burton, Lympstone); 14, 45, 63, 105, 118 & 120 (Edith Timperley, Ebrington); 28 (Joyce Barker, Baunton); 36, 37 & 48 (Miss M. Whiteman, Cirencester); 56 & 73 (Mrs Westmacott, Cheltenham); 69 (Edgar Smith, Cirencester); 78 George Brain, Northleach); 80 (Molly Wormington, Cirencester); 82 (John Holland, Cirencester); 83 (Grace Cuss, Cirencester); 99 (Mr. Halle, Siddington); 101 (Michael Barnsley, Cheltenham); 114 (Mr Boobyer, Bristol).

From other sources the author acknowledges the following material held in the Corinium Museum collections: Cirencester parish record books: 29, 31 & 32; John Topham Picture Library: 44; Wilts & Glos Standard: 88 & 113; Oxfordshire County Libraries (Henry Taunt collection): 96 & 119; Cricklade Museum for the transfer of the original of pl. 100; Real Photograph Co. Ltd: 102; Cheltenham Chronicle & Glos Graphic: 103; Lechlade Bookshop (Mr & Mrs Lever): 109. Mrs Lock and Miss Ellis of Cirencester kindly supplied and identified pl. 76. Plates 10, 42, 111, 116, 126 & 127 were copied from prints and original postcards in the museum collections.

Research for this volume produced the following material, generously loaned or supplied for inclusion: Basil Packer, Packer's Studios, Chipping Norton: 16, 21, 39, 43, 49, 53, 55, 58–61, 79, 104, 110, 122 & 125; Donald Emes, Wotton-under-Edge: 1, 3, 4, 11, 12, 64, 70, 74, 77, 81, 84 & 86; Horace Haines, Chipping Campden: 9, 23, 34, 40, 50, 51, 67, 68 & 124; Bledington Society through the good offices of Sylvia Reeves: 26 (courtesy Mrs D. Harvey); 117 (courtesy Mrs M. Painting, Daylesford); 121 (courtesy Rupert Harris, Icomb); and 123 (courtesy Cecil Acock); University of Reading, Institute of Agricultural History and Museum of English Rural Life: 17–20, 24, 25, 30, 47, 62 & 85 (with information kindly supplied by Mr. Andrews, Willersey); Bingham Library, Cirencester: 15, 27 & 108 (Cox Collection); 57 & 91 (J.H. Thomas Collection) and 72; Heather Shuttlewood, Kempsford (courtesy Edwin Cuss, Cirencester): 33, 41, 128 & 131; Philip Griffiths, Cirencester: 38 and jacket illustrations; Cheltenham Art Gallery and Museum: 90 (courtesy Mary Greensted); Jonathan Nicholas, Ampneysheephouse: 13, 22, 52, 75, 112, 129 & 130; Norman Irvine, Cirencester: 46, 65 & 71 (courtesy Wilf Harvey, Cheltenham); Mrs D. Day and Shelagh Lovett-Turner, Chedworth: 35, 54 & 107; Bob Sharp,

Stow-on-the-Wold: 66; David Hicks, Guiting Power: 87 (Information courtesy Mrs Ray, Cold Aston); W.C. Fallows, Northleach: 89 and for other Northleach photographs not reproduced here; Glos Constabulary: 115 (reproduced with permission of the Chief Constable); Author's collection: 92 & 95 (courtesy Humphrey Household); 93 & 97 (National Monuments Record); 94 (Stroudwater, Thames & Severn Canal Trust, courtesy David Boakes); 98 (Stan Gardiner, France Lynch with information from Brian Hillsdon) and 106 from a postcard.

Plates 5–7 are from the publisher's collection.

In addition, the author would like to thank Joe Henson (Guiting Power) and Sidney Jacques (Fairford) for answering specific queries so promptly, and Alan Welsford, Librarian of the Bingham Library in Cirencester for providing access to the local history collections in his care and facilities for study. Chris Bowler and Graham Light of Abbey Studios, Cirencester undertook the considerable task of copying from originals with their usual care and cheerfulness, and all the staff at the Corinium Museum tolerated with generosity the author's occasional diversions in pursuit of each new 'lead' during one of the busiest years in the museum's history. Cotswold District Council's commitment to the future preservation of the historic photograph archive should indeed be acknowledged and the author would always be pleased to hear of other Cotswold material for loan or inclusion in this permanent record.

To my wife Linda I owe more than customary acknowledgements; she has applied pressure and comfort in equal measure whilst the preparation of this volume has competed with so many other diversions and commitments. I am equally indebted to Samuel Carr of Batsford for a similarly sympathetic response to my apparent dilatoriness.

Introduction

The photographs in this album recall a quite different world from that of the present day; a quieter pace and a more contemplative approach are apparent, there is less concern with change and the rate of development is slower. This much is now a commonplace view of the late Victorian and Edwardian period up to the First World War. Rural as well as urban society experienced a great shock during the war years and many of its customs and traditions were irrevocably changed or vanished completely.

This collection is concerned with a rural area of great individuality. The Cotswolds are now presented to the visitor as if uniformly moulded, a pleasant landscape of stone walls and stone-tiled roofs to picturesque cottages set in an undulating landscape. The harsh reality of rural life in the later nineteenth century is, however, a key theme linking many of the scenes in this album; living conditions for rural labourers and their families were always simple and frequently sub-standard. The daily toil was indeed just that – an unremitting cycle of labour and family responsibility with only very rare breaks for relaxation beyond the church and the pub. Hence, for example, the constant popularity of the annual Whitsuntide Club Days in Cotswold villages – an amalgam of traditions linked together around a significant holiday date in the farming calendar (118). Equally, the village band offered relaxation of its own kind and a chance to mix with others in neighbouring villages and towns (123–4).

The farming cycle was constant, its programme of change within the rural scene reflected here in the selection of activities on the land. Tasks then often required many labourers (and other willing pairs of hands) – work which today is performed by the farming equipment we take for granted. Although often posed for the photographic record, such jobs as sowing or 'fiddling' seed by hand (16) and the sharply-remembered childhood experience of bird-scaring (18) typify a complete way of life. The effects of a lifetime of constant toil are also only too well detailed (as in 24–5).

There is always argument as to the correct delineation of the Cotswold region; without doubt its heartland is the high ground between Cirencester and Moreton-in-Marsh, extending north and west to Broadway, Chipping Campden and Winchcombe. In fact the Cotswold scarp presents a long face to the Severn vale all the way from the northern outliers of Bredon and Meon hills southwards as far as Bath. The dip-slope to the south and east is marked by river valleys flowing largely to the Thames and (in the south-west) into the Severn, and this is another characteristic of the area – an open hill or wold landscape broken up by particularly attractive river valleys.

And it is the stone which creates uniformity; a limestone ranging in colour from the cream of Bath through a wide variety of greys and yellows to the warm golden-orange of the north-east Cotswolds, running into Oxfordshire and Northamptonshire ironstone country. This raw material has always been worked to good effect, for buildings, walls and architectural ornament.

This volume confines its range largely to the Gloucestershire Cotswolds, extending occasionally into west Oxfordshire and south Warwickshire, very little if at all beyond Wotton-under-Edge in the south-west and hardly anywhere off the scarp of the hills into the vale of Severn. Gloucestershire as a county, of course, is not a geographically uniform area, and even to the inexperienced eye divides quite easily into the Forest of Dean west of the Severn, the vale itself as a central backbone from north to south, and the Cotswold uplands forming more or less the whole of east Gloucestershire. It is this latter area which the selection of photographs reflects. In modern administrative terms this is almost totally the area of responsibility of one authority, Cotswold District Council, and of the 113 parishes within this authority about one-third are represented here.

Drawing together a volume of this kind suggests two further thoughts. The first is the constant and ever-accelerating loss of personal recollection of the scenes reproduced here, not only by the generation which remembered the years before the First World War but now too their sons and daughters. Research work during the gathering of much of this material led in almost every case to a blank absence of information created by the passing of an older member of the community. The compilation of the written record for future generations is equally as important as the preservation of the original photographs themselves.

The second thought is how much valuable photographic record remains in the care of families to whom it has been entrusted. An increasing awareness of the historic significance of such items is welcome and this should ensure a greater hope of preservation. However vigilance against casual loss is a constant preoccupation of collectors, museums and record offices.

The publication of many more historic photographs has emphasised the quality of some of the everyday work of small one-man studios in country towns all over Britain. The boom in photographic production in the years immediately before the First World War has left a considerable body of work ranging from the indifferent to the excellent. This modest contribution includes work from all across the range, but the quality produced consistently by the Cotswold Publishing Co in Charfield and Wotton-under-Edge (not least the result of the collotype printing process for photographic material) is worthy of record, and the collection gathered by Donald Emes in Wotton-under-Edge includes a number of examples of this company's production (1, 3, 11, 84, etc). Amongst the individuals, W. Dennis Moss of Cirencester stands out as consistently good value (42) and it is a matter of great regret that his fine collection has not survived intact to form the archive it so richly deserved.

Better fortune has characterised the 'County Life' series taken in the north and east Cotswolds during the first decade of this century by Percy Sims; this was absorbed into the studio of Frank Packer at Chipping Norton where much of the original archive survives intact (see for example 21, 39, 55 & 58). Thomas Taylor at Chipping Campden (40, 51, 124, etc), J.W. Gardner at Fairford (75) and C. Powell also at Fairford (128, 131) are represented here, some of their work surviving through a mixture of good luck and family inheritance. Although not a photographer by profession, Jack Lawrence at Chedworth had no mean ability with a camera and pl. 54 of himself is one of a fine collection of family portraits, largely of his delightful sisters, taken by this amateur enthusiast.

There is much which the photographic record can tell us of people of an earlier generation and places now fast changing. Although it might be argued that the Cotswolds as a region has changed relatively little in the past half-century in comparison with other areas, it is the author's hope that the subjects contained within this volume will show that change is indeed ever present and no less so within a rural community in the Gloucestershire countryside.

The photographs in this album have been selected from the following parishes, all in Gloucestershire unless stated:

Alderley 86
Aldsworth 27
Andoversford 65
Bampton, Oxon 122
Bledington 26, 79, 117, 121 & 123
Blockley 127
Brimscombe 98
Broadway, Worcs 7
Burford, Oxon 8 & 62
Charlton Kings 83
Cherington 52
Chedworth 35, 46, 54, 71, 82, 101,
    103 & 107
Chipping Campden 9, 20, 23, 40, 44,
    50, 51, 67, 68, 119 & 124
Chipping Norton, Oxon 104
Cirencester 2, 15, 28, 29, 31, 32, 36,
    37, 42, 48, 69, 72, 76, 78, 80, 88,
    100, 102, 108, 111–3, 126 & 129
Coates 91 & 97
Coln St. Aldwyn 13 & 75
Condicote 10
Ebrington 14, 45, 118 & 120
Fairford 30, 33, 41, 125, 130 & 131
Hatherop (?) 110
Hasleton 87
Ilmington, Warwicks 34
Kemble 92
Kings Stanley 24
Lechlade 96 & 109
Mickleton 105
Northleach 73, 89 & 114–6
North Nibley 84
Painswick 3 & 11
Salperton 38
Sapperton 19, 25, 90 & 93–5

Towns & Villages

Cirencester Town Hall

2 **OPPOSITE** Cirencester: market place, town hall and parish church – a focal point of activity (c.1905). The cattle and sheep markets once held in the centre of the town were moved to a new market in 1867, although implements, etc., continued to be sold as here. Amongst the items on offer is a sail-reaper probably by Samuelsons, the Banbury manufacturer. The pump, trough and weigh-bridge can also be seen

3 **ABOVE** Painswick, with a typically Cotswold high-pitched gabled building in the centre and the Bell Inn sporting an impressive sign for Smith & Sons 'fine Brimscombe Ales and Stout'

4 **BELOW** Tetbury Market House (c.1900), the focal point of the town since the mid-seventeenth century and one of a number of such buildings in the centre of Cotswold towns. The covered area served as both a meeting place and a market

5 South Cerney *c.*1890, recorded by the Oxford photographer H.W. Taunt. The road is not metalled and is correspondingly muddy; most of the buildings are traditionally roofed in stone slates, although one barn remains thatched, a rather more common feature of the district then than it is today.

The wayside cross marks the junction of the village's two main streets; its stone ball and iron cross are interesting (and perhaps later) features

6 The village of Stanton consists largely of one main street running up to the foot of the Cotswold scarp. This peaceful scene pre-dates the motoring age in one of the most architecturally distinguished of the smaller north Cotswold villages. Seventeenth-century additions of globe and sundial embellish the medieval shaft and base of the village cross (*c*.1905)

7 LEFT The Lygon Arms Hotel at Broadway, photographed by W. Galsworthy Davie whose splendid work appeared with E. Guy Dawber's text in *Old Cottages, Farmhouses and other stone buildings in the Cotswold district* (Batsford, 1905), capturing much of the distinctive character of Cotswold buildings.

The building appears in the parish registers as early as 1532 as the White Hart, and remained so until acquired by General Edward Lygon. Prosperous as a coaching inn, the Lygon fell on more difficult times once the railway network across the Cotswolds had become established, and only with the development of leisure motoring has it – and Broadway – regained its busy character

8 BELOW Burford Priory, derelict for 80 years from 1828 until restoration began in 1908. The original priory was a small Augustinian hospital recorded in the thirteenth century. Its remains were obscured beneath the first large house built on the site by Sir Lawrence Tanfield, in which he entertained King James I in 1603. William Lenthall, who later became Speaker of the Long Parliament, purchased the priory in 1637 and it remained in the family until 1828. The Lenthall coat of arms above the front door decorates the much altered three-bay façade. The cult of the picturesque in Burford, so well known to the modern visitor, really began in 1911 when E.J. Horniman purchased the priory and continued its restoration together with that of a number of houses in the town

9 RIGHT Church Street, Chipping Campden with the parish church of St. James, one of the best-known Cotswold landmarks. On the right one of the lodges at the entrance to the ruins of Campden House, built by Sir Baptist Hicks *c*.1613 and destroyed during the Civil War. In the foreground is the town's cart wash and going about his rounds the milkman for Stokes' Dairy in the town (*c*.1910)

10 BELOW At Condicote, an isolated high Cotswold village, the 600-year-old wayside cross has long acted as a focal point. Alongside is the village pump and the area behind a busy mixture of smallholdings and allotments (*c*.1910)

11 ABOVE New Street, Painswick (*c.*1900), the main through-road from Cheltenham to Stroud. The owner of the horse and trap is no doubt quenching his thirst in the Falcon Hotel

12 RIGHT Activity in Market Street, Wotton-under-Edge outside the Swan Hotel, including the establishment's own waggonette. A 1907 advertisement called the Swan 'one of the best and most comfortable in the district', with passengers met from every train calling at Charfield station on the Midland Railway

13 Dean Row, actually in Coln St.
Aldwyn parish but almost in Hatherop
village. Probably all occupied by estate
workers, this group reflects the humbler
Cotswold vernacular building style, with
dormer windows providing a first-storey.
Demolished by 1907 and replaced by a new
group of cottages

14 The main street in the north Cotswold
village of Ebrington, with a high proportion
of thatch on both barns and cottages
(c. 1900)

People

15 OPPOSITE Right Hon. James Henry Legge, Baron Sherborne of Sherborne in the County of Gloucester, Lord of the Manors of Bibury, Aldsworth, Eastington, Sherborne and Windrush (1804–83). Land ownership in his family extended to over 10,000 acres in the county, plus the patronage of the parish of Sherborne with Windrush

16 ABOVE Using an aero fiddle or seed thrower on a Cotswold farm. Time-consuming and laborious, this method often supplemented mechanical drilling

17 LEFT A breast plough on a small-holding at Shottery, Stratford-on-Avon. Thigh-pads protected the user, who pushed the plough forward, its metal blade paring the turf. Once used for turning the shallow soils of Cotswold fields, the breast plough continued to be useful for small or steep areas and cleaning-up operations (c.1911)

18 Bird-scaring in the fields to protect the growing crops. Many a small boy or girl spent lonely and chilly hours in the fields for only a few pence a week, armed with a clapper made of two boards, a couple of pebbles in a tin or just their voices and hands to keep the birds off the corn. In Winchcombe the pay is remembered as twopence a day or one penny and a swede

19 Thomas Fisher, farm labourer at Sapperton, recorded in 1868 at the age of 106. No doubt recalling earlier days, this study shows the all-purpose smock in use, worn here with woollen stockings and no trousers

20 Mr. Hedges of Chipping Campden, a shepherd

21 'A modern milkmaid' (in the words of the photograph's original caption) and her favourite Shorthorn cow. This was a very typical scene with the three-legged stool and the pail the only 'tools of the trade'. The Dairy Shorthorn was a popular milking breed throughout the country but could never achieve the milk yields of the later imported Dutch Friesian which today virtually dominates the English dairy industry

22 OPPOSITE Feeding the farmyard chickens (*c.*1914). Most farmer's wives kept a number of chickens as an additional income and source of food. Note the well-established rick yard, each rick thatched for protection through the winter months

23 OPPOSITE BOTTOM Feeding the turkeys in a Cotswold farmyard near Chipping Campden. The lady's pinafore remains spotless; or was it produced especially for the photographer? In the yard a well-filled rick has been thatched for protection against winter weather

24 RIGHT TOP John Brinkworth, who worked as a hedger and ditcher in and around Kings Stanley

25 RIGHT BOTTOM Jonas Workman, a roadmender at Sapperton, and his wife Esther

26 John and Mary Hall at a point-to-point at Bledington Grounds. From a well-known family in the village, John (born in 1838) worked at University Farm for the Stow family for 61 years as a 'carter and day-labourer' and was presented with his long-service certificate by the Chipping Norton Agricultural Society. When the old age pension was introduced in 1908, John was moved to tears at the prospect of accepting such charity saying he would earn 'as long as there was earning in him'. His wife was well-known as a bonnet-maker for women in Bledington and Stow and for 25 years gave the church a thorough weekly clean for sixpence

27 Robert Garne of Aldsworth (c.1892), when he founded the Cotswold Sheep Society to preserve this rare breed. Once a common sight on the Cotswolds, the breed had been reduced to one pure flock of sturdy animals weighing up to 300 lbs with a thick fleece and a characteristic forelock covering the face

28 John Arkwell Bridgeman (1842–1916), a bachelor
and one of seven brothers, lived in Cirencester all his
life. Taking pride in his appearance as a well-dressed
man about town, he must have been a walking
advertisement for his employers, Hyde & Co., General
Drapers and Silk Mercers in the Market Place

29 Mr. A.F. Whatley, an earnest churchman and one of the two original churchwardens at Holy Trinity Church, Watermoor, Cirencester, which was built by Sir George Gilbert Scott in 1850/1 to serve the growing southern part of the town. Watley continued to hold office for many years and died in 1903 at the age of 100

30 Mr. Robert Kimber, who for 26 years was sexton at Fairford Church and died at the age of 85 in February 1910. He is holding a cane fishing rod used to point out details of the fine stained glass windows in the church; the rod is still used for this purpose. On the wall behind hangs a framed slate used as a noticeboard for baptisms, marriages and funerals; the impressive wooden gates have now been replaced

Some Ciceter Ringers *In memorial* *Terry 1908*

31 The Band of Ringers of Cirencester Parish Church; a commemorative photograph following the ringing of a peal on 29 May 1907 ('Oak-apple Day') at 6 a.m. under the terms of the will of Mrs Pardoe of Cheltenham to celebrate 'the happy restoration of the Monarchy to England'. Seated at the front is H. Hughes 'the veteran ringer aged 87 years who, although he now does not take the rope in change ringing, climbs the steps two or three times every Sunday to chime the bells for the services. The last occasion in which he rang in a peal was on December 31st 1868 in a peal of grandsire triples of 5,040 changes in three hours and two minutes.'

29th May was the birthday of Charles II and the day when he entered London at the restoration in 1660; its name recalls the king's concealment in an oak tree after the battle of Worcester in 1651

32 Mr. Teal 'a constant worshipper at Matins', in Cirencester (*c.*1900)

33 Mr. Bewlay, 'who lived in Fairford through five reigns' (c.1910)

34 The third Earl and Countess of Gainsborough at Foxcote House, Ilmington which was their home for a number of years. The Noel family had held the lordship of the manor of Chipping Campden since the seventeenth century and were created Earls of Gainsborough early in the nineteenth century. Campden House was greatly enlarged by the first earl, whilst the third spent much of the family's resources on the building of Campden's catholic church, completed in 1891

35 Delaretha Lawrence at the age of 15 at Chedworth with baby Mabel Parry in 1905

36   The Infants Class at Powell's Endowed School, Cirencester, about 1907; a study in discipline and concentration. The schoolroom boasts the limited educational aids of the day supplemented by a windowsill decoration of wild flowers. The lucky child on the rocking horse is Edith Bridges, and the teacher Miss Travers

37   Teacher Miss Polly Smith's class I at Powell's Girls School, Cirencester in 1910–1, each child shining like a new pin

38 Village schools at Salperton (*c*. 1905), forming part of a row of cottages. Perhaps the bicyle belonged to the photographer?

39 'A rest by the way' is the contemporary photographer's caption: three farm workers take a break from their labours. Heavy-duty cord trousers, gaiters and hob-nail boots attest to hard physical work in the fields

40 Pomp and due ceremonial in Chipping Campden *c.*1910. The mayor, George Ebborn, is flanked by his macebearers Harry Ellis and William Izod, the latter a particularly long-standing Campden family name. Of its four town maces, two dated from 1605 in silver, and a further two in silver gilt were the gift of the lord of the manor in 1773

41 Mr. Geech of South Farm, Fairford with his family in his new Ford, one of the first in the area

Farming

42   Taking a break from the heavy task of
cultivating in Cirencester Park (*c*.1910). This
team of oxen was well-known in the district
and were bred at Cirencester until 1964

43 Turning on the headland, this three-horse team is breaking down the ploughsoil. Both men wear the ubiquitous waistcoat and gaiters

44 OPPOSITE TOP Court Farm at Chipping Campden, with the parish church in the background. Although this view probably dates from the 1920's, it is very much a period piece, with barns and stables grouped around the yard, and a thatched lean-to on the right. The waggon is typically Cotswold and almost certainly was made and used locally throughout its working life

45 OPPOSITE BOTTOM A ploughing match in progress at Ebrington c.1900. Although such occasions offered companionship and entertainment, they also had a serious purpose; farming developments in the eighteenth century produced new types of implements, and competitions of this kind allowed plough-makers to assess the quality of their products in comparison with their rivals. Matches also offered a ready form of publicity for new products, and these groups of farmers and labourers seem intent upon the competition

47 RIGHT Carrying home faggots on a Cotswold farm. Although no other details are known which might give this photograph its location, the wagon is a very distinctive example of the Cotswold type, with a prominent 'bow' rave rising over the high rear wheels. Together with the short 'ladders' attached fore and aft to the body, this gives greater height to the loads which the wagon could carry. The yellow and salmon pink colour scheme was a further distinctive feature of this regional type

46 ABOVE Collecting faggots in Chedworth woods on the Earl of Eldon's Stowell Park estate c.1910–11. The team comes from Church Farm at Yanworth. With the first horse is carter Harry Waring, with the second his son Charlie, and the third Thomas Parrot. The other men also come from local village families, virtually all of whom worked on the estate

48 ABOVE Haymaking on the lawn at Watermoor House, Cirencester, home of Mr. Thomas Kingscote after his move from The Abbey. Kingscote was appointed in 1893 to the ancient and honourable office of Gentleman of the Cellars to Queen Victoria; he was also a staunch churchman, being one of the first and most active members of the Sunday Lay Movement ('in Favour of Sunday Rest and Worship'), and is here entertaining the Dean of Rochester and his wife, Mrs. Storr. The staff are from left to right: Mr. Belcher (head groom), Charlie Butcher (under coachman), Mr. Boulding (butler) and Mr. George Whiteman, Kingscote's gardener 'and faithful friend' from 1908–19. On the hay cart is Billy Woods, formerly the butler

50 Mowing in the hayfield near Chipping Campden on land used by Mr. Dick Smith (standing on the right with his dog Rover). Although this picture was taken c.1920, it represents a very typical farming scene, with the ubiquitous two-horse mowers widely used all over the country

49 BELOW A study by the north Cotswold photographer Percy Sims showing the full range of activity in cutting hay: a mower, a hay-rake, and plenty of helpers with hand-rakes to gather in (c.1910)

51 Mr. Brotheridge and his companion scything in the hayfield near Chipping Campden, c.1910. A systematic approach to the task produced best results, with groups of mowers working in unison across the field

52 Mr. J.R. Smith of John Smith & Son, forage merchants of Cirencester, buying grain directly from the fields at Cherington

54 OPPOSITE Jack Lawrence with a Marshall portable engine threshing at Manor Farm, Chedworth, *c*.1907. This engine travelled around the farms on Lord Eldon's Stowell Park estate

53 Building a rick using horse-gin and elevator. The hay-rake gathers up remaining material. The wagon is of the 'boat' type – a shallower version of the traditional harvest wagon

55   A threshing scene on the Cotswolds with two sets of tackle in use and a third set just in view. This is no doubt contractor's equipment being moved from farm to farm

57 OPPOSITE BOTTOM A group of barns and rick yard at Church Farm, Siddington, with the spire of St. Peter's Church rising behind. The tithe-barn in this group is believed to date from the thirteenth century

56   Soldiers of the Forage Department of the Army Service Corps baling from a rick on a Cotswold farm during the First World War

58 OPPOSITE TOP Hay stored in ricks was often sold directly off the farm, its removal undertaken by itinerant hay-trussers who used hay knives to cut from the rick in sections to form into trusses, using a manually-operated and portable hay press. Often two men formed a team cutting the hay and working the press; each truss weighed approximately 56 lbs and was pressed and tied into shape ready for transport

60 Shearing sheep by hand – a classic scene before the introduction of mechanical clippers. Perhaps these men preferred the traditional method. Behind, the farm buildings are well-maintained

59 OPPOSITE BOTTOM 'Bringing home the orphan', says the photographer's original caption. The state of the fields and the farm tracks is obvious from the cart wheel and the legs of the donkey

61 'Ready for the show': a full turn-out for this pair
of horses with brasses and decorative ear-covers
(*c.*1908)

Markets & Shops

62   The Midsummer hiring fair in Sheep Street, Burford, the annual occasion (until 1914) when farm-workers sought new employment and landowners new men and women. It was long customary for both indoor and outdoor farm servants to be engaged by the year. Sometimes called 'mop' fairs, these occasions were enlivened by a pleasure fair to be enjoyed by all on a rare day free from work

63 OPPOSITE TOP Opening day of the new cattle
market at Winchcombe, 15 February 1905. Farmers
cluster around the sale ring and only the auctioneer
enjoys any shelter. Emerging from the ring are the
first two bulls to be sold, both Shorthorns. This large
dual-purpose breed was by far the most popular
breed of cattle at the turn of the century, and
included a widespread genetic variation. Some strains
were heavier milkers, whilst others proved better
beef cattle, as here. The division of the breed into
Beef and Dairy Shorthorns broke down the genetic
variations, which might otherwise be playing a vital
role today in replacing the imported dual purpose
breeds from the Continent

65 Market day at Andoversford, *c.*1909. Central to
the Cotswolds and an important junction on the rural
railway network, this was a popular meeting place for
the farming community

64 OPPOSITE BOTTOM Inside the Wotton-under-Edge
office of Fred Fry, F.A.I., Auctioneer, Valuer & Estate
Agent, Mortgage and Insurance Broker in the early
summer of 1904. The firm also had offices at Stroud,
Dursley and Berkeley

66 OPPOSITE TOP Stow Fair (*c.*1905), one of several markets or street fairs held in Cotswold towns since the middle ages. Stow owes its layout as a town to the establishment of a 'port' or market there in the twelfth century. Late in the fifteenth century, the granting of two annual sheep fairs instead of one underlined its importance; by 1750 over 20,000 sheep were usually sold at each fair. Subsequently Stow Fair became better known as a horse fair and here a large number of horses are lined up along the Fosse Way. Agricultural implements are also for sale

68 Leaving the sale pens at Chipping Campden market (*c.*1904) and no doubt bound for the abattoir of one of the town's butchers. In the centre stands the Town Hall, a medieval building largely rebuilt early in the nineteenth century and beyond the more famous Market Hall built by Sir Baptist Hicks in 1627 and intended for the sale of cheese, butter and poultry

67 OPPOSITE BOTTOM Market day in the Square at Chipping Campden, held on the last Wednesday of each month. The name Chipping means market and the town was an important centre for sheep sales, a weekly market and three fair days per year being confirmed as early as 1247. The sheep enjoyed pride of place in the town centre with cattle and pigs in a paddock at the rear of one of the main hotels. This well-attended sale shows a very typical group of local farmers and landowners following the auctioneer's progress

69 OPPOSITE TOP D. & J. Smith, a long-established butchery business on this site in Black Jack Street, Cirencester since 1808 but founded elsewhere in the town in the later eighteenth century. Six generations of the Smith family have been Cirencester butchers. Daniel, the third generation, is the 'D. Smith' of the left-hand side in this view (c.1880); his sons Daniel (b.1849) and Jesse (b.1851) are the 'D. & J. Smith' of the right-hand side of the shop. Another brother was a butcher in Fairford. Jesse wears a bowler and stands second left. He succeeded to the business when his brother emigrated to New Zealand and subsequently remodelled the premises into a single frontage of true Edwardian character; this remains today as a welcome feature amidst the aluminium and plastic. A pillar of the local community, Jesse upheld the nonconformist traditions of many tradesmen and was treasurer of the Congregational Church for over 30 years. As a fine judge of cattle he served at Tetbury Fatstock Show for 25 years and once at Smithfield

71 Mr. Perry and his family setting off on his rounds from his village shop in Chedworth

70 OPPOSITE BOTTOM J. Richings' shop in Long Street, Wotton-under-Edge c.1900: 'Bacon Factors, Butchers, Cheese Factors, China Glass and Earthenware Dealers, Corn Dealers, Coal Merchants, Dairymen, Grocers, Hauliers and Hurdle Makers.' A fine display of hams and turkeys complements no small amount of sawdust on the pavement!

72 Demolition of dealer W.P. Paish's shop at 77, Castle Street, Cirencester *c.* 1907–10, some time after it appears to have gone out of use. The fine gabled building next door had been converted into one of Cirencester's first garages in 1901 for W.G. Bridges and this expansion preceeded a later move to new premises further down the street. Note the careful stacking of roof tiles for re-use

73 Messrs Wane, draper and grocer in Northleach
market place, pre-1889. One of the ladies in the group
is Miss Clara Maretha Soul the milliner

Rural Trades & Industries

74 W. Arthurs' deliveryman making a sale outside the Regency toll-gate house at the top of Rushmire Hill, above Wotton-under-Edge (c.1900). Both the brake and the drag shoe are in use at the top of this pitch. The ornate gothic house was occupied by staff from the nearby big house after the turnpike was abandoned; its occupants enjoyed a clear view across much of the vale of Severn

75 RIGHT The village smithy at Hatherop on the Coln St. Aldwyn road and actually in the parish of Coln. The blacksmith here served a wide agricultural area with a constant flow of implements to repair and maintain

76 BELOW Samuel Jukes' iron and brass foundry in Watermoor, Cirencester in about 1912, remarkable for the number of men at work in this building. The two three-ton wheels were an emergency order resulting from a ship breakdown, and the whole job was completed within the required seven days – hence the photograph for the record. Working on the final touches are two felters, or trimmers of the finished mouldings. The owner stands by the door with his local carrier, George Cox, in the bowler hat

77 OPPOSITE BOTTOM The small family business of Lacey & Andrews, carriage builders of Wotton-under-Edge, with final work on a new trap

78 OPPOSITE TOP In the yard of the Nelson Home Brewing Brewery in Gloucester Street, Cirencester. The owner, Edmund John Price, was also a lime burner and quarry owner, dealing in 'building stone, road stone and stone tiles at the shortest notice'

79 Delivery to the King's Head Inn at Bledington from the local brewery. The horses wear protective ear coverings

80 OPPOSITE BOTTOM Workmen with the tools of their trade at Cirencester Maltings. In order to avoid bruising to the barley grains during the malting process, wooden forks and shovels were used, replaced in later years by mechanical scoops for turning and gathering the grain (c.1912)

81 OPPOSITE TOP A small brickworks off Gloucester Street at Wotton-under-Edge, with Wotton Hill on the skyline. Although the equipment reflects a modest concern, the evidence of extraction is considerable all over the hill-side

82 OPPOSITE BOTTOM Percy Holland, coal merchant of Fosse Cross – one of three small coal-haulage businesses which operated from the isolated station yard (c.1910)

83 ABOVE Setting off from Bafford Farm, Charlton Kings with the milk float of J. Jones. The dairy shorthorn herd graze in the paddock next to the farm-house, which is in timber and brick, contrasting sharply with the stone buildings of the Cotswold hills

84 ABOVE The pony and trap of James Talboys, dealer of North Nibley

85 Charles Andrews and his wife outside their cottage in Church Street, Willersey about 1900. The produce of Mr. Andrews' market garden included asparagus and his baskets contain some of the earliest vegetables to be grown on the Glebe ground in the village. The couple were married when Charles was 30 and his wife 60 and they lived in this cottage for 30 years; at her death at the age of 90, Charlie said 'she's been just like a mother to me'. Incidentally, his food and provisions for the day are carried in the rush basket or frail. The photograph was taken by the village rector, the Rev. C.O. Bartlett

86 RIGHT Monk's Mill at Alderley in the valley of the River Little Avon flowing south-westerly off the Cotswolds to the River Severn. This is one of a large number of woollen mills in the river valleys of the western Cotswolds and centred upon Stroud. The boom period for cloth production was the early nineteenth century, when many of the mills were rebuilt; thereafter the industry declined in favour of Yorkshire. Monk's Mill closed in 1869 and was derelict when this photograph was taken *c.*1905

88 ABOVE Selling boot laces in Cirencester cattle market (*c*.1908)

87 LEFT Edward Wheeler, who delivered mail by bicycle and later by pony and trap to Hasleton, Salperton and Compton Abdale. The post was brought from Cheltenham by the Northleach carrier and left in the postman's hut at Hasleton Pike

89 Workmen attracting an interested crowd of onlookers during the erection of a new line of double-post telegraph wires through Northleach in 1907. This line stood alongside the A40 across the Cotswolds for many years and formed a well-known landmark

90 Traditional building methods in use in the construction of a Cotswold cottage, possibly at Sapperton. This is significant as one of the small-scale domestic buildings – invariably in a rural setting – designed by the Arts and Crafts architects Ernest Gimson and the Barnsley brothers

Transport

91 OPPOSITE The derelict portal of the Sapperton
tunnel on the Thames & Severn Canal at Coates in
December 1912. Nearly $2\frac{1}{4}$ miles in length, the tunnel
has been described as the most ambitious engineering
feat of its day; it took five years to build and was
adorned with a portal at each end, one in the gothic
and one the classical style. Although overgrown and
collapsing, the details of the structure remain clear,
with a central pediment, flanking columns, one
rectangular and two circular entablatures, plus two
niches on either side of the tunnel arch. The effect is
an impressive entrance to a cold and dark journey for
the boatman! Stone figures of Father Thames and his
counterpart for the Severn, Sabrina – apparently
intended for the niches – remain no more than local
legend

92 Smerrill bridge or aqueduct carrying the Thames
& Severn Canal over the Cirencester-to-Malmesbury
road near Kemble. A single arched construction, and
notoriously leaky (according to those who travelled
regularly beneath), the aqueduct formed part of the
summit level – or reservoir – of the canal which
extended from Sapperton to Siddington, and linked
the Severn via Stroud with the Thames at Lechlade.
Opened in 1789, the canal suffered many vicissitudes
in the later nineteenth century and was closed
completely in 1933. This section was formally
abandoned in 1927. The picture was taken about 1914

93 The Oxford photographer Henry Taunt's timeless view of Daneway, Sapperton in 1904. This tiny community owed its origins to the Thames & Severn Canal, which had been constructed up the steep-sided Golden Valley to this point some years before the nearby Sapperton tunnel was completed. During this period Daneway was a focus of activity, with a new road cut up the hillside to link with Cirencester to allow canal goods brought from Stroud, the river Severn and beyond to be transported forward by road. With the tunnel completed, the canal opened to through traffic in 1789 and thereafter Daneway continued to provide a wharf and stopping-off point en route. On the right the wharf, wharfinger's cottage and store with just visible above the lock gates the entrance to the side pond – or reservoir – installed in the 1820s to help with water conservation along this section. Daneway top lock can be seen under the bridge arch; with the Bricklayers Arms pub on the left of the photograph. Still a public house today, it was built in 1784 by the canal contractor John Nock to provide accommodation for his workmen

94 Repair and restoration work on the Thames & Severn Canal at the western or Daneway entrance to the Sapperton tunnel. After a period of steady decline in the fortunes of the canal in the later years of the nineteenth century, a Trust formed from local authorities attempted restoration. This too was short-lived and Gloucestershire County Council took on the burden in 1900. Concentrating upon the all-important summit level in order to overcome water shortages, the restoration programme included concrete lining for some sections and renewed clay puddling for others. Here the contractor's plant is crushing clay for use on the canal bed close by; the tunnel is blocked off by wooden stop-gates (c.1903). This restoration was also a failure and the last working boat is recorded in 1911

95 The process of re-puddling the canal bed at Puck Mill short pound on the Thames & Severn Canal below Frampton Mansell in 1907. The canal was closed for three months from 19 August so that the work of digging new clay and ramming it down to form a new surface could proceed. The following year a further period of closure was necessary to fill with concrete a large hole which had appeared in the rock beneath the clay puddling. Apart from minor details, the process of work shown here was remarkably similar to the original construction techniques of the 1780s.

96 Preparing for the road from the Trout Inn at Lechlade – a study of a Thames-side inn by Henry Taunt in 1902

97 The Tunnel House Inn at Coates on the Thames & Severn Canal, photographed by Henry Taunt during an expedition westwards from the river Thames in 1904. Like its counterpart at Daneway, the inn was constructed as a lodging house for the canal's construction workers as the New Inn. The top floor was undivided and obviously served as a dormitory, whilst the ground-floor tap room was more than usually spacious. The building remained much in its original condition until a fire in 1952

98 ABOVE The *Humaytha*, a product of the boat-building yard of Abdela & Mitchell Ltd of Hope Mill, Brimscombe. A wide range of vessels were manufactured for clients all over the world and shipped into the river Severn via the Thames & Severn and Stroudwater Canals.

The 27-ton *Humaytha* was registered in 1905 for use in Brazil where its twin decks made it ideal for use as a river steamer

99 OPPOSITE TOP A group of contractor's navvies, probably employed on the construction of the Midland & South Western Junction Railway northwards from Cirencester to Andoversford Junction. This section was the final link of a through route from the LSWR at Andover northwards to the Midland Railway at Cheltenham and hence to Manchester, and was completed in 1891. The construction of this 12-mile central section was contracted to Charles Braddock of Wigan, who employed over 1000 men, lodging them locally and in camps along the route. Most were not local and retained employment by moving from one contract to another

100 RIGHT Scene at Cirencester (Watermoor) station of the M.S.W.J.R., which was opened as the northern terminus of the route from Andover via Swindon at the end of 1883. Services were provided by tank locomotives built by railway engineers Beyer Peacock of Manchester, and one is seen here with its crew. Also recorded are a group of contractor's workmen, probably preparing to start work on the northern extension of the line towards Cheltenham. If so, the date would be 1888, and perhaps the foreman standing on the left is Charles Braddock? Note that the workmen sitting on the engine have their trousers 'yorked up' – tied below the knee to give greater flexibility

101 OPPOSITE TOP Operations in hand to double the track of the M.S.W.J.R. north of the tunnel at Chedworth, part of the improvements to the through route carried out at the turn of the century

102 ABOVE Midland & South Western Junction Railway locomotive no 9, which played a significant part in the revival of fortunes of this impecunious concern following the appointment of Sam Fay as general manager in 1892. In comparison with other engines in the stock, this 4-4-0 tender engine was powerful (and grand) enough to form the mainstay of the new direct passenger express service from Cheltenham to Southampton – a key part of the MSWJR's fortunes. The engine cost £2,360 from Dubs & Co of Manchester, the money being advanced by one of the railway company's directors

103 LEFT A line-up of workmen at Foss Cross station on the MSWJR north of Cirencester in spring 1907. An isolated spot, the station nevertheless served a wide country area including the villages of the Coln valley, and no less than three independent coal merchants operated from the goods yard there. From left to right: A. Beams (porter), H. Dayment (fireman), R. Gillett (stationmaster), J. Bartlett (coal merchant), A. Mills (coal merchant), W. Smith (signalman) and Messrs Tilling (fireman) and Thomas (engine-driver)

104 LEFT Chipping Norton station on a peaceful afternoon, *c.*1910–12. Serving a market town and some local industry, this could be quite a busy station on the cross-country Banbury & Cheltenham Railway, opened throughout in 1887

105 OPPOSITE BOTTOM Maintenance and repair gang at the entrance to Campden tunnel, Mickleton on the Oxford, Worcester & Wolverhampton Railway, the 'Old Worse & Worse' as it was popularly known. The construction of the tunnel had been the scene of the 'battle of Mickleton' – a confrontation between rival groups of contractors' navvies which quickly entered railway folk-lore

106 BELOW Rail services in the Stroud valley had a history all their own, to cater for a large number of stops over a short distance. Self-powered steam railcars were introduced by the Great Western Railway between Chalford and Stonehouse on 12 October 1903 and the push-pull nature of this service survived until withdrawal in 1964. The railcars were immediately popular; 2,500 people tried them out on the first day and the G.W.R. estimated 15,000 passengers during the first week. Fitted steps allowed for stops at level crossings as well as stations – eight stops in eight miles with 23 minutes allocated for the journey. The cars were gas lit and presented a rather handsome appearance, with an oak frame and finish with external panelling in Honduras mahogany. The seating capacity was 52. This view at Stonehouse in 1903 partially shows the station shelter on the up platform, with distinctive chimney and other details from Brunel's original designs for the line

Social Life

107 **BELOW** Descending Chapel Hill from sunday
school at the Congregational Chapel in Chedworth in
1906. Much of this photograph is characteristically
Cotswold: moss-covered stone roofs and dry stone
walls contrast with some thatched barns and a small
rick-yard

108 **OPPOSITE TOP** Servants at The Beeches,
Cirencester, obviously a fairly well-to-do town house
(c.1890)

109 **OPPOSITE BOTTOM** The entire staff of Lechlade
post office, which served the town and surrounding
villages

110 OPPOSITE TOP A small village ceremony, but of significance: the first letter from the new village post-box. Is it at Hatherop?

111 LEFT Christmas 1908 presentation line-up of the Midland & South Western Athletic Club Band outside Watermoor station in Cirencester on the north-south route across the Cotswolds from Cheltenham to Swindon. The works at Cirencester was an important link in the working of this cross-country line from 1895 until absorption into the G.W.R. in 1924. James Tyrrell, a locomotive and carriage superintendent from 1903–24, was also vice-president of the band and is seated next to the drum. The band flourished for a number of years until the first world war

112 ABOVE Out for a ride in the family donkey cart, Mrs Lucy Smith, a farmer's daughter from Hatherop and the wife of the proprietor of John Smith & Son, forage contractors of Cirencester

NORTHLEACH — THE PRISON —

113 OPPOSITE TOP LEFT Part of the large crowd at the annual tea and meeting of the Cirencester branch of the Primrose League on 30 May 1912. A political organisation strongly Unionist in character, the League was well-supported in Cirencester with a membership of over 1100 standing for 'religion, the Constitution and the Empire'. The day was obviously successful; 500 guests sat down to tea at 5 pm followed by a gymnastics display and traditional sports, including the ever popular tug of war. Before the speeches, the crowd was entertained to a dancing competition with music by the Midland & South Western Junction Railway Works Band; thereafter the speakers concentrated their energies on attacking the Home Rule Bill in general and Mr. Lloyd George in particular; they were doubtless well received. All in all, a good day out for 6d (non-members 1/–)

114 OPPOSITE TOP RIGHT Police Superintendent Thomas Basson, in charge at Northleach from 1874 until his retirement about 1894, during which time he was assisted in his duties by Constable Whitehead. This studio portrait also shows his wife, who worked as a wardress attending to the female prisoners in the cells at the former prison buildings at Northleach

115 LEFT Gloucestershire Constabulary officers at Northleach police station about 1860, from an official police record

116 ABOVE 'The old prison' at Northleach, probably the dourest of all Cotswold buildings, isolated at the crossroads to the west of the town at the junction of the Fosse Way and the Gloucester–Oxford road (now A40). More correctly styled as a house of correction, the buildings were constructed on an hexagonal plan, enclosed by a high wall. Northleach was one of four such buildings erected in Gloucestershire in the 1780s as part of a programme of prison reform inspired by Sir George Onesiphorus Paul, high sheriff and magistrate. The architect, William Blackburn, designed cell-blocks around a yard, with day-cells on the ground floor and night-cells above; the keeper's house was centrally placed to oversee all activities both within and without. Intended for 37 petty offenders, the house of correction remained in use from 1791–1857, after which, with some rebuilding, the site was used as a police station and magistrate's court until 1974. The surviving buildings, including a cell-block, have been preserved as the Cotswold Countryside Collection museum of rural life

Entertainments & Leisure

117 Village line-up to celebrate Queen Victoria's Golden Jubilee in 1897 at Rosepool Barn (now the village hall) in Bledington. In the group is Parson Hartshorne, vicar in the parish for 43 years from 1871. Seated on the ground is Mr. Irving Senior the village schoolmaster

118 The Club Day procession forming up in Ebrington, c.1900. Most north Cotswold villages enjoyed an annual Club Day or Feast Day, involving virtually all the members of the village community. Daughters of village families who were working away 'in service' made an especial effort to return home for the occasion. At Ebrington the holiday extended to three days; the principal event of the men's dinner taking place on the first day, followed by a tea-party for women and children and on the third day an opportunity to visit friends and relations in the area. This Whit Thursday procession includes the main banner plus one banner each with the arms of Lord Ebrington and the Earl of Harrowby, the two major landlords of the village

119 Bidford-on-Avon morris dancers at a floral festival in the grounds of old Campden House at Chipping Campden in May 1896. The building was destroyed during the Civil War. Campden's morris men maintained (and still do) a long tradition of dances, each with its own peculiarities within the overall morris patterns. Photographs of the later Victorian 'revival' sides are not common and reveal that the dress varied between each dancer, although the fiddler, the fool and the hobby horse can be easily identified

120 RIGHT Sitting by the fire in the Ebrington Arms, Ebrington, still the village pub and originally a seventeenth-century farmhouse

121 Bledington Band of Hope annual outing to Sarsden Lodge on 10 August 1905. The use of a farmer's harvest waggons was traditional and this is an excellent example of a Cotswold type with a light body rising high over the large rear wheels. These belonged to Mr. V.V. Conroy of Fifield, At the tea, the temperance band might play and Jonah Hunt, farmer and temperance supporter, would produce his portable boiler to help provide tea. His wife made dolls as prizes for the girl's three-legged and other races

122 A Band of Hope or other children's group-
outing in the Bampton area. Three splendid Cotswold
wagons provided the transport (*c.*1905–10)

123 Bledington temperance band on the occasion of the wedding of one of its members, April 1909. Such bands grew out of the need for leisure activity 'away from the pub' as part of the temperance movement, and the Bledington band formed later than in many other Cotswold villages. Strongly associated with the Methodist chapel, its numbers were largely drawn from long-standing non-conformist village families. From left to right: **BACK ROW:** Tom Acock, Frank Acock, H. Cook; **STANDING:** C. Hall, T. Slatter, C. Slatter, J. Stayt, W. Hall, George Acock, Harry Slatter, Oliver Acock, Ernie and Lewis Hall; **SEATED:** Alf Stayt, John, George and Reg. Stayt, W. Andrews, . . . **FRONT ROW:** F. Stayt, Fred Hall, George Viner and Cecil Acock. The bearded figure on the right is Jonah Hunt of Rectory Farm, Methodist, special constable, school manager, parish councillor and great supporter of the band

124 Chipping Campden town band *c.*1910. At the back Fred Hathaway and Arthur Bunting, and seated Fred Bennett, Charlie Downer and Jack Webb

125 The procession at Fairford Carnival, 8 July 1909, the ship's complement of HMS *Dreadnought* recruited from students at the Royal Agricultural College in Cirencester

V. W. H. [Earl Bathurst's] Hounds, Cirencester.

126 OPPOSITE TOP The V.W.H. (Earl Bathurst's) Hounds at the Kennels in Cirencester Park, c.1900. *'It is as a hunting centre that Ciceter (Cirencester) is best known to the world at large, and in this respect it is almost unique. The "Melton of the West", it contains a large number of hunting residents . . . and the country round about, from a hunting point of view, is good enough for most people. Five days a week can be enjoyed over a variety of hill and vale, all of which is "rideable".'* (J. ARTHUR GIBBS, A Cotswold Village, 1898)

After 1886 the Vale of White Horse Hounds were divided into two packs, the original pack going to Cricklade whilst Lord Bathurst built up his pack at Cirencester. With neighbouring hunts, there was a regular and well-observed programme of hunting. Monday was the day for the Duke of Beaufort's hounds, riding 'the best of the grass' in stone-wall country. Tuesday saw Lord Bathurst's pack close to Cirencester and Wednesday the Cotswold Hunt making good speed over its stone-wall territory. In contrast the Braydon Forest and North Wiltshire fenced landscape provided the bill of fare for Thursday and Friday, with a further variation for Saturday enthusiasts

128 ABOVE A meet of the otter hounds at the Swan Inn, Southrop prior to working the waters of the river Leach

127 OPPOSITE BOTTOM A good turn-out for the North Cotswold Hounds at Northwick Park, Blockley

129 Turn-out of horses for show in Cirencester Park by John Smith & Son, forage merchants of Cirencester. The central figure is Raymond Smith who died in 1903, the same year as his father, the firm's founder

130 Fishing in the River Coln near Fairford, a famous trout stream (*c*.1903)

131 With the catch of coarse pike from the waters of the Coln at Fairford, a protection for the trout fishing of this famous river

BURFIELD

ACACIA STREET - 8 JAN 1993

ST. AUDREYS 2 2 AUG 1996

FRIENDSHIP HOUSE 2 7 NOV 1998

"OAK COTTAGE" 7 - JUL 1999

- 6 OCT 1999 ACACIA STREET

MEAD HOUSE 2 3 DEC 1999